D1501829

BLAZERS®

Hidden Worlds

WITHDRAWN

BEHIND THE RACKS:
EXPLORING THE SECRETS OF A
Shopping Mall

by Tammy Enz

Reading Consultant:
Barbara J. Fox
Reading Specialist
North Carolina State University

Content Consultant:
Daniel Jasper
Director of Public Relations
Mall of America
Bloomington, Minnesota

CAPSTONE PRESS
a capstone imprint

Public Library

Blazers is published by Capstone Press,
151 Good Counsel Drive, P.O. Box 669, Mankato, Minnesota 56002.
www.capstonepress.com

092009
005619WZS10

 Books published by Capstone Press are manufactured with paper
containing at least 10 percent post-consumer waste.

Library of Congress Cataloging-in-Publication Data
Enz, Tammy.
    Behind the racks : exploring the secrets of a shopping mall/by Tammy Enz.
    p. cm. — (Blazers. Hidden worlds)
    Summary: "Describes the behind-the-scenes places of a shopping
mall" — Provided by publisher.
    Includes bibliographical references and index.
    ISBN 978-1-4296-3386-4 (library binding)
    1. Shopping malls — Juvenile literature. I. Title. II. Series.
HF5430.E69 2010
381'.11 — dc22   2008054996

Editorial Credits
Jennifer Besel, editor; Bobbie Nuytten and Veronica Bianchini, designers;
    Eric Gohl, media researcher; Laura Manthe, production specialist

Photo Credits All images by Capstone Studio/Karon Dubke except:
Shutterstock/Andre Blais, cover; Shutterstock/Andreas Bjerkeholt, throughout (concrete texture);
    Lagui, throughout (paper with tape); Pokaz, throughout (grunge); prism68, 6 (mall); Robyn
    Mackenzie, throughout (torn paper); V. J. Matthew, 5 (mall)

The images in this book are from several different malls.

Table of Contents

Chapter 1
Secret Stops............................ 4

Chapter 2
Authorized Personnel Only 8

Chapter 3
The Hidden Mall 26

○ ○ ○ ○ ○ ○ ○ ○ ○ ○ ○ ○ ○ ○ ○

Glossary............................... 30

Read More 31

Internet Sites........................... 31

Index.................................. 32

CHAPTER 1

SECRET STOPS

Shoppers stroll through the mall, looking for hidden deals. They have no idea that the mall hides other secrets too.

LEVEL 1

Bloomingdale's

East Broadway

South Avenue

Macy's

East Parking

West Parking

Underwater Adventures Aquarium

Amusement Park

West Market

Travel Station (Lower Level)

North Garden

Sears

Nordstrom

SALE
UP TO
50%
OFF

BOXING WEEK SALE
ENTIRE STORE

BLACK'S

Visit us on the third level.

Behind the stores at the mall, there's a world few people see. Come explore the places hidden from shoppers.

INSIDE INFO

The two largest malls in the world are both located in China.

CHAPTER 2

AUTHORIZED PERSONNEL ONLY

Stockroom

Beneath the mall is a city of products. In the **stockroom**, workers steer **forklifts** through underground streets. Workers stack and sort the thousands of products stores sell.

stockroom — a room for storing supplies
forklift — a vehicle used to move heavy loads

INSIDE INFO

In large malls, the stockroom can be as long as a football field.

EMERGENCY
EXIT

5 M.P.H.
SPEED LIMIT

INSIDE INFO

Some older malls have back hallways that
no one uses anymore. Workers might not
even know about them.

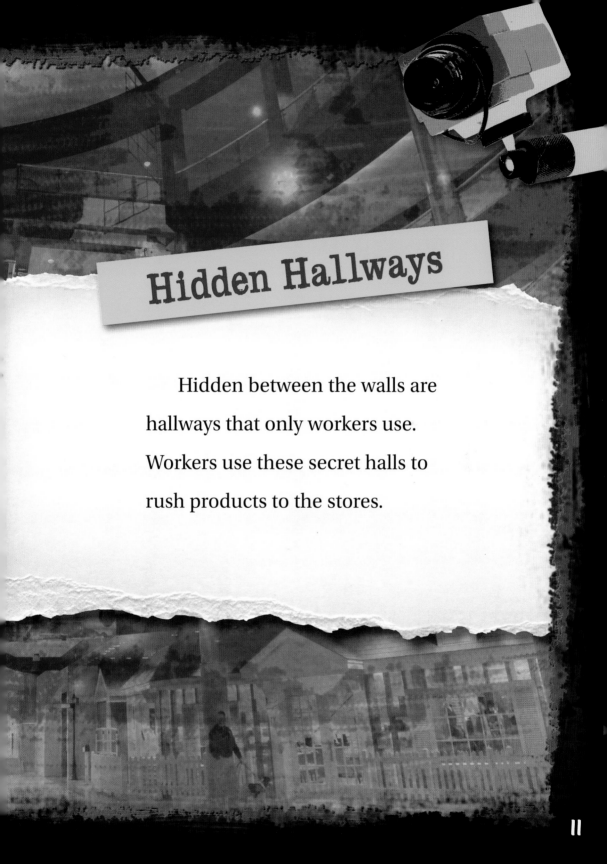

Hidden Hallways

Hidden between the walls are hallways that only workers use. Workers use these secret halls to rush products to the stores.

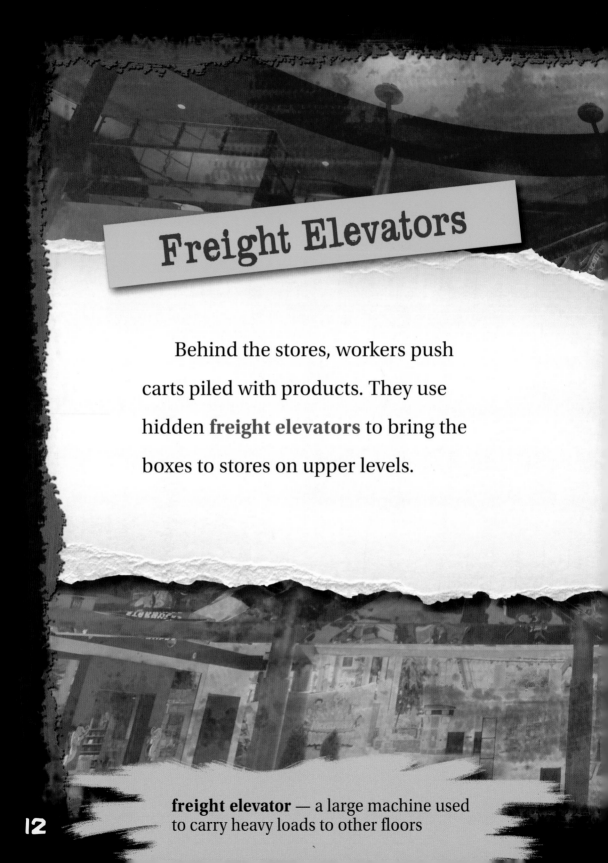

Freight Elevators

Behind the stores, workers push carts piled with products. They use hidden **freight elevators** to bring the boxes to stores on upper levels.

freight elevator — a large machine used to carry heavy loads to other floors

freight
elevator

INSIDE INFO

Malls recycle leftover food from restaurants. One large mall sends leftovers to a farm for pig food.

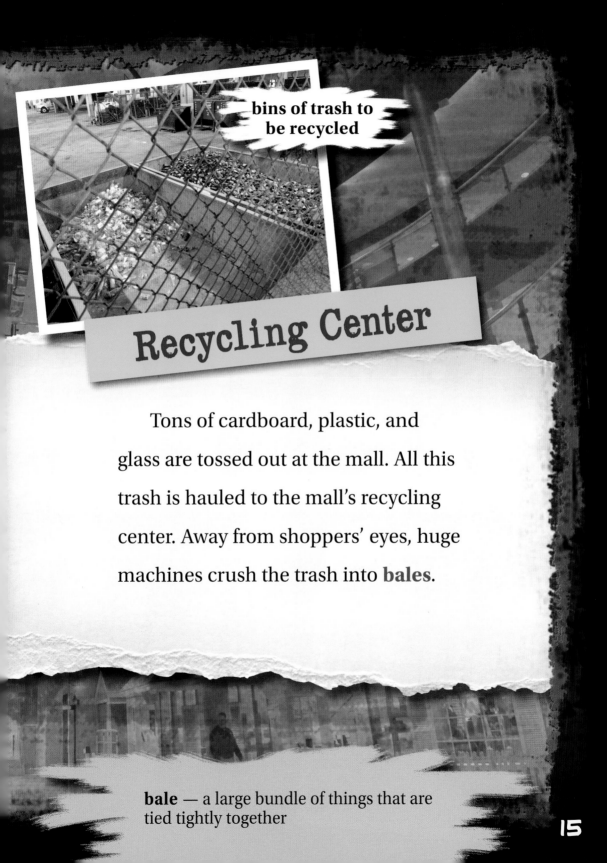

bins of trash to
be recycled

Recycling Center

Tons of cardboard, plastic, and glass are tossed out at the mall. All this trash is hauled to the mall's recycling center. Away from shoppers' eyes, huge machines crush the trash into **bales**.

bale — a large bundle of things that are tied tightly together

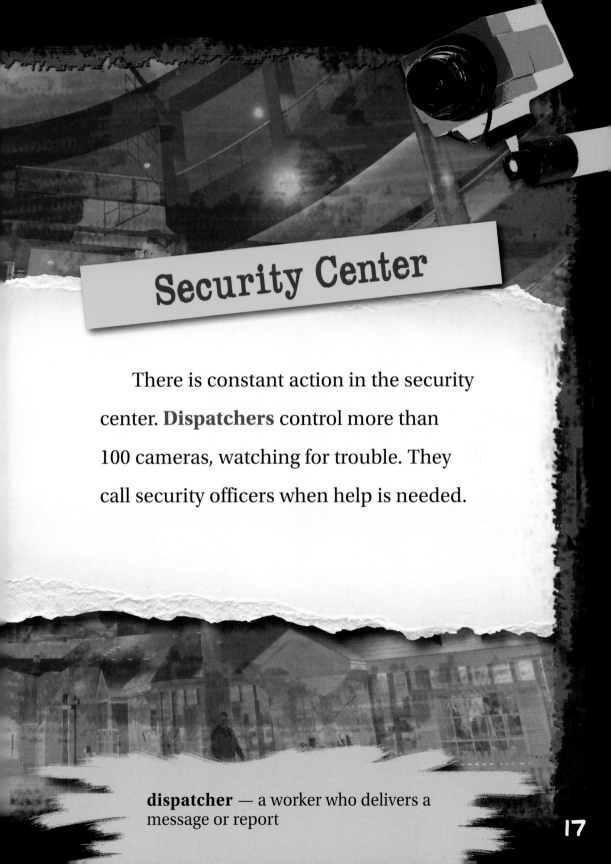

Security Center

There is constant action in the security center. **Dispatchers** control more than 100 cameras, watching for trouble. They call security officers when help is needed.

dispatcher — a worker who delivers a message or report

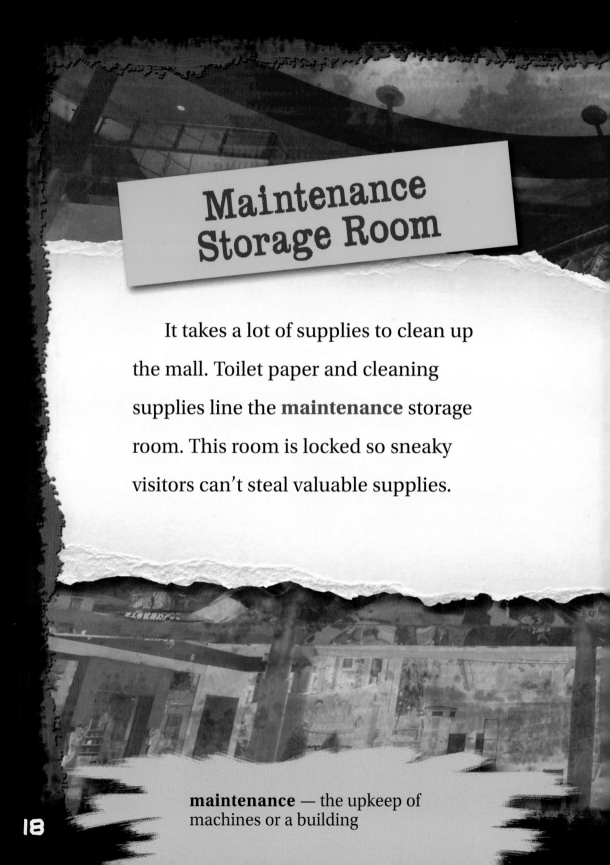

Maintenance Storage Room

It takes a lot of supplies to clean up the mall. Toilet paper and cleaning supplies line the **maintenance** storage room. This room is locked so sneaky visitors can't steal valuable supplies.

maintenance — the upkeep of machines or a building

supplies in the
storage room

INSIDE INFO

Big malls use more than 7 million rolls of
toilet paper each year.

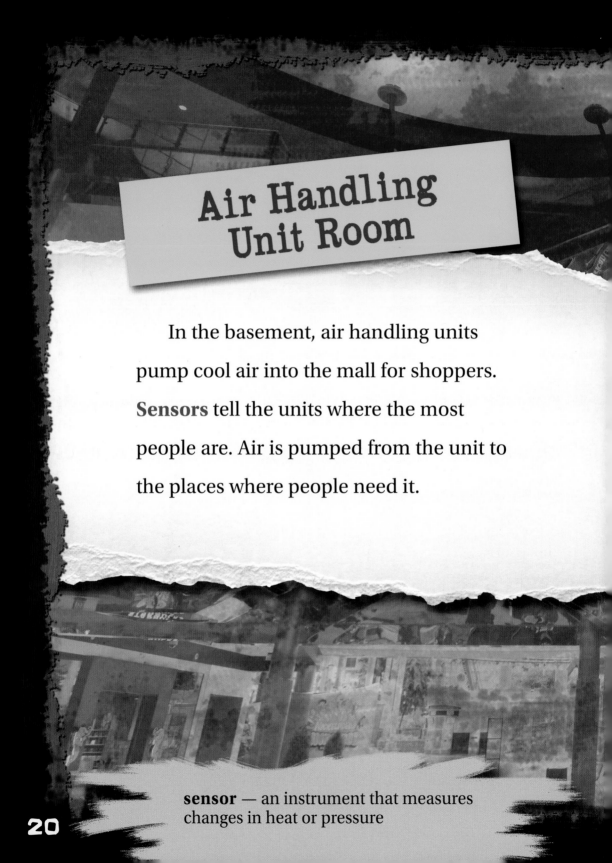

Air Handling Unit Room

In the basement, air handling units pump cool air into the mall for shoppers. **Sensors** tell the units where the most people are. Air is pumped from the unit to the places where people need it.

sensor — an instrument that measures changes in heat or pressure

air unit
gauges

box that controls the
flow of electricity

Electrical Room

Behind a heavy, locked door, the electrical room keeps the mall running. Electrical cables stretch through the walls to every store. All the lights, phones, and cash registers run on these cables.

ELECTRIC ROOM

DANGER

HIGH VOLTAGE
KEEP OUT

Jewelry Vaults

Vaults hidden behind some stores protect jewelry and money. No one can open the vaults without the secret codes. Most workers never know their store's code.

vault — a locked room or area for storing valuable items

vault
lock

THE HIDDEN MALL

Locked rooms and secret hallways are all around the mall. These hidden places keep the mall running smoothly.

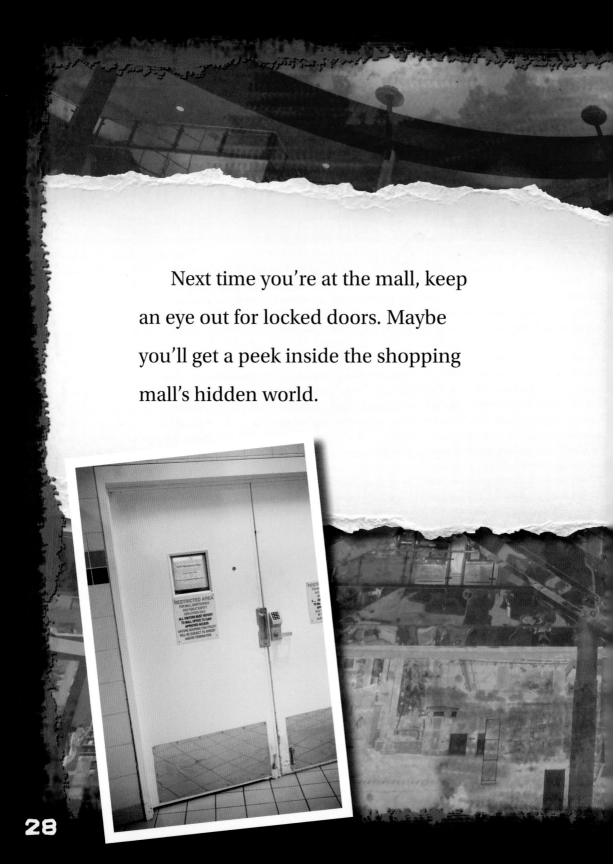

Next time you're at the mall, keep an eye out for locked doors. Maybe you'll get a peek inside the shopping mall's hidden world.

INSIDE INFO

Some malls recycle water from their air conditioning system. They use it to flush the toilets.

GLOSSARY

bale (BALE) — a large bundle of things that is tied tightly together

dispatcher (DISS-pach-uhr) — a worker who delivers a message or report

forklift (FORK-lift) — a vehicle with two forks at the front, used for lifting and moving heavy loads

freight elevator (FRAYT EL-uh-vay-tur) — a large machine that carries heavy loads between different levels of a building

maintenance (MAYN-tuh-nuhnss) — the upkeep of machines or a building

sensor (SEN-sur) — an instrument that can detect changes in heat, sound, or pressure, and sends the information to a controlling device

stockroom (STOK-room) — a room where products or supplies are kept

vault (VAWLT) — a room or area used for storing money or other valuables

READ MORE

Enz, Tammy. *Under the Lights: Exploring the Secrets of a Sports Stadium.* Hidden Worlds. Mankato, Minn.: Capstone Press, 2010.

Gorman, Jacqueline Laks. *The Shopping Mall.* I Like to Visit. Milwaukee: Weekly Reader Early Learning, 2005.

Sarver, Amy. *Science at the Mall.* Everyday Science. Washington, D.C.: National Geographic Society, 2004.

INTERNET SITES

FactHound offers a safe, fun way to find Internet sites related to this book. All of the sites on FactHound have been researched by our staff.

Here's all you do:

Visit *www.facthound.com*

FactHound will fetch the best sites for you!

INDEX

air handling units, 20

dispatchers, 17

electrical rooms, 23

forklifts, 8
freight elevators, 12

hallways, 10, 11, 26

jewelry vaults, 24

maintenance storage
    rooms, 18

recycling, 14, 29
recycling centers, 15

security centers, 17
security officers, 17
sensors, 20
shoppers, 4, 7, 15, 20
stockrooms, 8, 9
stores, 8, 11, 12, 23, 24

trash, 15